T0150622

A SLEEPLESS MAN SITS UP IN BED

ANTHONY SEIDMAN

A SLEEPLESS MAN

SITS UP IN BED

EYEWEAR PUBLISHING

First published in 2016
by Eyewear Publishing Ltd
Suite 333, 19-21 Crawford Street
Marylebone, London WIH IPJ
United Kingdom

Cover design and typeset by Edwin Smet
Author photograph by Robert Lopez
Printed in England by TJ International Ltd, Padstow, Cornwall

All rights reserved
© 2016 Anthony Seidman

The right of Anthony Seidman to be identified as author of
this work has been asserted in accordance with section 77
of the Copyright, Designs and Patents Act 1988
ISBN 978-1-908998-53-8

Eyewear wishes to thank Jonathan Wonham for his very generous patronage of our press.

Eyewear Publishing is grateful to the Instituto Nicaragüense de Cultura for its permission to publish 'Funeral Song On The Death of Joaquín Pasos' by Carlos Martínez Rivas, as translated by Anthony Seidman.

WWW.EYEWEARPUBLISHING.COM

The word (שמים)
'Heavens' *means*
'Carry water,'
'there is water,'

'fire and water'

which He mixed one
with the other
and he made of them
the heavens.

from Rashi's commentary
on Bereshit (Genesis)

Table of Contents

for Nylsa

Transmission

A jungle, a small jungle, the size
of a hummingbird-heart or crab-nebula
witnessed through an Arizona telescope the girth
of a blue whale's lungs; a jungle
only I can hear: its rustle of fronds, ant
mandibles scissoring leaves
which will raft phalanxes across the river
and into the bush, ox-carcasses scattered and
picked to the bone; a jungle with its thunder
as rain clatters on the canopy
covering this page; a jungle,
no larger than a toddler's tooth,
yet teeming with beetles, rills,
spider-monkeys, irritable tarantulas, termites;
it is a jungle I taste in the manner
a boy extends his tongue in a snowfield,
and flake lands on tongue's tip and
twilight is like voices reverberating
through amniotic fluid into an embryo's sleep;
a jungle I savor as fruitful, fluvial, tang of lemon,
lifetimes of salt, a fountain of milk,
a tributary, the blossom of a wet dream;
this jungle which you too
apprehend, like a man smelling lust
in the pores of a female flushed with estrus,
the way a woman tastes the stiffened nerves
in a boy awakening to puberty like
fanged fish flitting through warm currents –
this, the jungle I bequeath you. It is the genius
jungle, the genus jungle, the shaman's feather,
and the word's ovulation. It is the only
jungle that matters. The emerald
flash between two immemorial nocturnes.

9

Fable of a Wolf, a Lyre, & One Million Inhabitants

Listen my brother
About the ugly city
All the tarpaulins concealing bones and bent nails
And the acacias rotten and the pigeons
Crapping on the statue of Benito Juárez
The avenue through the desert
Where the wolf dumps the gutted women
And the wind gagging on dust
And the fat
Heat lolling under awnings, sucking shade
Oh my friend my brother
The world could fit in a crystal bowl
But still there would be windows to smash
Yet the sour light in August
Does not botch the singing
Of your drunkenness
Brother there are crows in our joy
And the vinegar of your verse
The tumbleweed scampering down *calle cobre*
And the litter
And the wind-swept, bursting
Scraps of litter!

Affluent

This river opens between the pages
of a journal wherein children color
itineraries for crows, or the shoes belonging
to parents buried beyond the smokestacks.
This river twists, froths a glossolalia, currents
slap against rocks, and the river
rises, spreads greenness across this page.
Men wading into this river sniff
the mud that sticks to the fur of lost dogs,
but they also taste a tooth perforating the gums
of a toddler whose mother has placed him
on the parlor floor, as she fills a pot with water
that had traveled a recirculation
from sierra precipitation, then
became rain driving into a tributary that
now leaps its banks, floods this page,
recedes, sinks into the damp clay of spring,
snakes a trajectory through pipes and
gurgles from out her kitchen faucet. This river
quenches the thirst of stones, stretches
up cliffs so that those who believe
in miracles behold a waterfall, calligraphy
of mist. This river is the cloud river, the blood
river, the white river that zigzags through
the emptiness between letters, the vortex
humming between two dependent clauses. This is
the river that soothes the saintly and mad,
river that runs alongside those who can no longer
walk, but keep faith in the charity of locusts,
the nutrients in dirt, the cosmos
ringing inside the almoner's empty cup.

The Trilobite

This Cambrian-thru-Permian
eras invertebrate, crawled

& burrowed in shallow ocean stretches
for millions of years,

feeding on organic ooze &
particles from sea-floor,

legs pushing nutrients
into his mouth also propelled

him thru sediment.

Trilobites were lovely,
with a chitinous armor

that resembled the lines &
interstices on a Mondrian;

as with modern lobster,
crab, they seasonally

shed their shells, leaving
amateur & paleontologist with

thousands of effigies like
sedans rusting & overtaking vacant lots.

Coatlicue, Whose Name Means 'Serpent Skirt'

Keeper of bone-keys
unlock my
ribs, and reveal
red spider spinning her web.

Angel of hallucinogens, mistress
of anesthesia, venom's
courtesan, castrate me, eat my
foam, slit afternoon from my wrists.

Lady of sulfur,
stir my heat
that I may hatch eggs
of a salamander.

Lady of clay
shatter my pitchers.

Lady of thirst
hone your blade.

Lady of stone,
noon has erupted, tart with dust.

Three slatterns wait
in the temple atrium;
their breasts are pendant, and they
unleash this rain of milk

as I enter you so that
we become the girl
who bled her father from every phallus,

whose dancing makes
the poet write afire
the priest skin the cadaver,

and man sweat his birth anew.

Decency

Tomorrow
when the Banker regurgitates
a pound of gristle
a coin of chilled marrow
an ingot of congealed fat

when he shivers
and vomits bile

and crows develop
a keenness for human meat

tomorrow
when the billboards and towers burn
and the Banker chokes
on the last of decent and
renewable resources: oxygen

and the clouds and precipitation and
the torrid chemistry of trout pushing upstream
not to mention the lungs in a poem or the growth of whiskers
            and decay of leaves

that moment of reckoning
that lull between two thunderbolts
that hiatus when the river stands up before plunging into
            the estuary

what unbridled fire
will take up residence in the fist of a man who knows only
the verb of a machete's strike?

Mezcal

Guelaguetza festival, Oaxaca;
midnight in the zócalo.

After the red
spider of thirst
scratched
down my throat
& wove
her web of acid,
I drank a bottle.
The salt film before
my eyes
peeled:
shadows turned to smoke,
a bloodstream of color
sprayed
in the boom
of fireworks,
the faithful
raised
bottles while
fingers of xylophone
dug
into my eyes,
plucked daylight
from memory –
thus, unblinded,
I stumbled by
the Zapotec women who
genuflected
before a tree,
poured libations for
man-root,
woman-fish,
and the prodigal dead.

Hunger

I sleep like a family without a father, an orphan who clutches the fingers of his mother the color of ivy. Hinge clicks open, and crows are unleashed, staining the page black. I write what shatters, a goblet or the cool shell of a snail. After rain, earthworms are untied, and the earth opens her jaw so that I can imagine the congealing liquids in the iris of a dead dog. I spill open, like spiders stretching from the silk-sack eggs, or hair wafting of a drowned virgin, her skin peeling against the teeth of icy water. Because it rains inside the poem, and I cup my palms during this downpour, yet don't gather enough to wash the dirt from my sleep. Hungering, emaciated like a candle burnt to the wick, I discover language, stale and with as much sweetness as a piece of bread, with as much nourishment. Slice of bread can't feed a family.

Making the Pact Outside Chihuahua

It was a bus stop, and past midnight
at a 24-diner with smoke
basted on tile walls, and vats of pork
boiled in red chili sauce.
I stepped outside; light sped towards
me from stars and supernovas. A rust-
flavored wind stirred cobalt clouds,
and lightning cracked the night, struck
where sky meets earth, where black
touches black, and becomes neither.

On De Kooning's *Woman I*

Woman smeared in grease, brush-strokes of red,
Blue of uncooked meat, saffron, the black
of fingernails after an afternoon of changing car oil,
all scooped out and scribbled on canvas
edges. He painted your skin all the luster
of lard, spat rouge only on your nose,
no nipples on your breasts, plastic bags
once filled with soda water now sucked dry.
But through that mess you smile –
five fangs chiseled dull as horse teeth –
you flaunt your overbite, saying:
what if you stick your tongue at me,
I'll bite! And your eyes, the mud basins
of the Mississippi, yet wide open, glaring
at the one who had the nerve to paint you.
Leather shining on a General's
boots would not make you blink.
With a shopping bag in your right hand,
clothes iron in the sinister, you're armed lethal,
ready to wrestle all of Manhattan's taxis. Fueled
with combustive mezcal, you look me
in the eye the instant before you open
the crystal door to Saks Fifth Avenue.
And you're ready for a bargain, you're thrilled
to live on credit. Your feet, goat-hooves,
click in midair.

Reaching the Step That Doesn't Crumble

Between stars and bread,
between the click of a light switch,
and the bulb's white flash,
between the taste of salt
and waves folding foam on the shore,
(around the bend of a coastal hill),
between this or that, and
between the between which resounds in this chant,
the cherry ripe in the brain,
the panting of a man running in his sleep,
fishnet swollen with a catch of air,
twig-snap thundering in a canyon,
and a basement perched on the shoulder,
and an attic rumbling in the stomach,
there is a word which can be peeled,
there is an odor sweet as a dead goat,
a color blinding as a lemon,
and all that passes through my brain
as I sit at this desk is like
a breath whirling between
5 o'clock and the universe,
where clouds litter leaves,
and a rain falls up from the earth to
plant swallows on the branches of this tree.

God Torments the Barren Once Again

After Joaquín Pasos

Evening in Juárez. The cantinas, empty.
A taxi stuffed with American soldiers crackles over gravel.
It is the hour of the leaf-storm
when homeowners lock their doors and
the childless, aging young woman
steps out into the street,
rips open her blouse so that
the wind will hone her breasts like volcanoes.

Admit Him, Admit Him

He knocks at my door, midnight.
What do you want? I ask
the keeper of thunder & diesel badlands.
I have no beer, & the heater's shot.

That wrinkled one stuffs
teeth into his lips, & growls:
*I'm your shadow, your interminable night
and my gullet's simmering acid…*

I step back & invite him in;
his fingers of vinegar stick thru
my chest, pickle this gristly heart so that
crows will caw at noon.

Xipe la Segunda

on a photograph by Manuel Álvarez Bravo

Because a drop of water creates amoeba,
insects floating in the embryo of their universe
and fish flitting at the edge
where water touches air but is neither,
because a drop of water turns into a lake,
because a drop of water is
the Milky Way and a water lily floats
and mud cools the shore,
your eyes rustle ferns
as you stare at Xipe the forever mother,
because you breathe,
and now step out into the light which at once
turns from black and white into sunshine and
green shade beneath palm trees,
because you approach Xipe,
stretch-marked hips and her navel
the scar of two ripped apart,
because you will lie down with her,
and the eyes behind your chest will open,
and the sun inside her womb will rise,
because a man and a woman are a drop of water,
because Xipe is sex fusing with sex,
because Xipe is stone striking sparks against stone,
she hands you her dress to toss on the ground,
as lizards sun themselves and then scatter,
and lianas curl around the bough.

Two

1

Mosquito, the hours
you live suffice.
Moon without wings.

2

Blue blue of the sky, radiantly coquettish—
when I stretch up I feel you just within reach.

The Uncapped Pen

Between these words, a jungle: lianas curl around a stone deity, half-serpent, half-whore, with granite hummingbird feathers as a crown, and clawed feet. Gnats, mosquitoes and shade bullet-shot from white sunrays, and the humid stink, like the feet of cheese vendors in the market. Every frond of palms I brush open reveals a cliff's edge, and at the bottom, clouds roll slowly, dragging un-fallen rain. The deity sometimes speaks to me, here, at the peak of this tropical Himalaya. Drums drums I beat, but no clouds reach me. I decipher this jungle stone by stone because only the myopic can gaze into the star beneath the sun. Lianas move in wind and stroke her granite thighs. Drums drums I beat, waiting for rains to word. When they fall, the sun bursts in another hemisphere, frost thaws, and a hiss escapes from her granite lips—a wordless prayer for the jungle between words.

Jewel of Thirst

The door of fire is a harpsichord of blood.
The door of fire is palm leaves thrown supplicant at the hooves
       of a goat.
The door of fire is hope in a maguey thorn.
The door of fire is a needle threading water through the
       eye of a camel.
But you are a door of fire with your stomach of wheat,
You with your tongue of mud,
You with your fingers of rain,
You with an ax splitting open the sun,
You with your feet of milk,
With your breasts of ivy,
With your eyebrows that rustle at night and weave a frond
       for the moon,
With your eyes the color of lion's mane.
Oh world forever eaten by thirst,
The door of fire is water and
Words brimming over with a sky no birds contain.
Oh thirst never slaked by life,
The door of fire is Time that spawns, suckles, then devours me.

Vermeer

Even the dust and spear of straw on the kitchen floor are visible. The milk-maid pours a silken thread, clotted at the pitcher's mouth. On the table, loaves of wheat bread varnished by the gold of memory, while she gazes down at her chore, muscles around her elbows straining from the pitcher's weight. Behind her is a white wall, yellow-spotted, with one nail and its microbe-thin shadow. Outside the canvas, I only have patience to paint a nude with a few brush strokes, but Vermeer includes the stitches on his maid's mustard-colored blouse. And he brings me back to slow light drifting after love, when her red hair burns against the white pillow; he brings me back to a boyhood afternoon where I sit by a window, feel sun on my back, and watch dust-specks pirouette in a weightlessness older than the first apple falling from the bough.

Yucatán

The road to Yucatán stretches
between an ant's
bread-crumb burden
and a ripe melon,
between the moon frozen
at noon, and the stone
that bakes in my palm,
through the sun that
rises from under my shadow
and is peeled in an onion.

To taste the Yucatán:
ferns and palm trees in
the yawn of a spider,
fanatical whims of the hummingbird,
fruit card painted lime, a stallion
with a hard-on, milk
in the sponge, and
a mouthful of wasps.

But the road to Yucatán is only
the road.

The road to Yucatán is
feather, bean,
vine, and dust;

the road to Yucatán is
indelibly indelibly
erased

from a map drafted tomorrow.

Why I Stick My Arm Into the Earth

Because the Ant Queen is my mother;

the Ant Queen is my wife;
                    I praise
the Ant Queen,
                    I loathe
the Ant Queen
                    because
I adore her the way
I adore what bloats with putrefaction,
what smells of milk, what sucks marrow from boilt-bone,
what blooms under the butcher's fingernail,
what pierces, what lays
a brown egg onto the lapel of delectation,
what is buried, then dug up, and shaven with a black tongue,
what gestates in the belly round with quivering meat; because
the Ant Queen is amniotic fluid I once gargled, is yellowness
          oozing from a fork'd yolk,
plasma erupting from a deep burn,
              the Ant Queen
is ripped skin, the bleeding, and twilight of brain;
              the Ant Queen
is the basement stuffed with eyes,
& She waits;
She nests beneath dry Californian soil color of parched hickory
          chips, or corn-
kernel-flecked turd;
              the Ant Queen,
whose mandibles crunch open & shut, sounding like heavy
          scissors cutting a stack of
matte-paper;
              the Ant Queen,

whose eggs dribble from her gaster, larvae sheathes puss-soft
        and white like a toe's callus
after one has swam for an hour, liable to tear if picked at;
She, whose legs can rip in two the exoskeleton of a beetle,
        yet whose gait is as soft as the
letter H in Castilian;
She, whose eyes are a multitudinous rattle of sparks that shake
        in the fist of the gambler;
She, whose cardiovascular system is a tree of electricity,
        a torch of hydrogen, a
gravitational tug between such disparate nouns as parachute
        and shoe-polish;
the Ant Queen
who is my whetting-nurse,
and my purse and curse,
my minstrel and mistress of my nemesis, she reigns
from her mud-roof tunnel, she reigns,
cushioned atop her pyramidal hoard of eggs;
the workers mill, antennae knitting into antennae, like the
        hand-shaking of small business
            owners at a convention, of frat brothers at an
            all-nite kegger;
the workers mandible-haul the inch of pizza crust, a pill bug
        curled into a crescent,
mute agony of a centipede, its legs scintillating hopelessly,
        ketchup-smeared
scrap of napkin from Grease-Spoon, raisin, toothpick speckled with
diced coleslaw cabbage, cornbread crumbs, pencil shavings;
the workers delighting in the human debris, the backwash
        of what man squeezes dry,
the discarded, excreted, puckering black eye of ass, and pipes;
all for the Ant Queen,
who is my wife and left me for a free union with Andre the Giant,
who is my left toe when I break Matzoh,
who is my molar crumbling communion's cookie of a panic attack,

30

who is my skin when seen through the glass skull of a
          semiotic hyperbole, who
simply shot-put
is the logos at 5 o'clock when all the bulls have stained
          the sand crimson
when the man doesn't hunger the Chinoiserie of spiral jellyfish
but the pulmonations of an ox, leaf-storm, swarm of ants
          at the zenith of summer,
the hard lungs swollen with dumb air and the red gnats
          that rupture the eyeballs of a
stallion in heat,
while She pisses
her runny rice-ooze of eggs eggs egg eggs
while she hisses aroused,
incubating her load, bubbles bursting in the rupture of every egg,
with the prayer that is the paroxysm of matricide, of
a hot blade into the labium, lightning slicing a tree,
with the word,
with the lips that once cut open to suck in a wider decibel
resound their meaty walls with the weight of the moon,
with the bloodbath of syncretism,
with the scream cauterized.

I Come from the Tribe of Clouds

My words pour
sleet or fire.

The Earth is hard
but below me.

On Modigliani's Portrait of Diego Rivera

Corpulent and jocund, you grin
in a mahogany parlor the color
of a gourmand's coil of excreta
after glutting on steak and merlot.

Your melanin glows in red-
Earth the texture of chitin. Now you chuckle,
Like the face of an omnibus passenger
half-riant before the jerky window frame.

Why? Because you are gorged
with the sap of the pimp,
with the honey of the Pentecost,
with bedroom eyes of Buddha,
with the burp of a lecher sated after his lunch...

And despite murals rising above factories,
colors mixed in denim and steel,
colors to eviscerate the pipes of capitalism,
despite the happy mustache of Stalin,
you were, and are in this portrait, a playboy
in heat, well-dressed, and piggish.

Where Source and Shadow are Fused

To travel at the speed of light
you must become sun chafed
under the weight of a stone,
air glistening in a rope
of water unraveling from a clay jug,
and noon's sizzling flash on
cars rattling over potholes.
It is not enough to harvest
protein from a plum, gather
desire from the sandaled feet
of a woman across the aisle on a bus,
and reach the speed where angles
of a square become round, and
a circle is the straightest line
to reach where source
and shadow are fused. To travel
at the velocity of moonlight,
and with the ardor of crab-nebulae,
you must learn how to
inhale water, and drown in
that black liquidity when
the ladder of milk had just
reached your lair of sexless
hydrogen and dust. Only then,
like the flitting of hummingbird,
whir of atoms unlocking in granite,
grumble of shifting faults erasing
your glimpse of the earth's homecoming
from molten core into helium cloud, only
then will you learn: light pulls you from sleep
so that together you knock down
these walls of static and meat.

On Two Canvases by Motherwell

1

The face of night is not
always black;
behind its shut eyelid, under
its ripped tongue, beyond
its mouth which sucks the gravity
of collapsed stars, there is
a streak of ochre,
there is a wink of scarlet like
flesh under nail,
there is at last
a rupture and blackness froths and
spindrifts and swallows that light again,
but there was a
tumult and redness streaked
across its face with
the profanity of brilliance.

2

Across the canvas of a Mexican night, black
monoliths slowly

lumbering, scarlet spindrift and
conflagration of liquor

itch of insomnia
trigger's click

(plucked bass string on
guitar reverberating like nerves during fever)

beneath the splutter of fireworks & agitated moon
the cacique

with rosy gunshots
riddled

In 2300 BC, Emperor Yao

Beheaded
his royal minister
who
drunk with courtesans
behind rice-paper screens
forgot to
warn his Lord of
an eclipse.
Thus
in the thinning
summer, I write
between steel-blue sky
and sand where tarantulas breed,
and search
for an omen that
will fix the moon
with the roaming, black
dog of my heart.

Disturbing the Peace: Always a Carnival

In unpaved *colonias* of Mexicali, celebrants rent jukeboxes, karaoke neon, and beer froths 'til five in the morning. Party-goers drive off in sudden lurches of buffalo-sized tires, bottles and splutter of sparks, and roosters soon rile up a ruckus.

Mud-lot cinemas of Bangkok: mothers chatter and feed brown nipples to gurgling gums. Men gamble and smoke from the back benches. On the screen an actress cries and wanders avenues leading to discarded sets: cobblestones from Medieval Paris or rural Colombia, Shangri La, snow-frosted plastic pines, russet buttes of Styrofoam.

A man hears up to 180 decibels without eardrums rupturing, while leaves' rustle during the green and soporific stun of summer peaks at 10 decibels, more hushed than the 20 decibels of a whisper in the dark.

There are languages that best pitch delight, grief at decibels which would perturb the average American. He'd cup his ears as village Turks ululate and clang pots during an eclipse, or stolid peasants collapse, shrieking when Mother's coffin is lowered into dark Antillean soil.

Like pneumatic drill, a rock festival zooms to 150 decibels, and that night when I was sixteen, Pixies on the stage awash in blue tarantulas and scarlet star-sparkles, teenage wave thrusting through electric heat, and I looked up, straight up, the argent moon-fields, and further off, the bloodspot of Mars, Jupiter, imagined the boulders of frozen ammonia, crags of jagged carbon-dioxide in Saturn's rings, crashing

against each other silently, rendered to smithereens in the vacuum where, had it have been possible for those Monkeys in heaven to thunder a guitar solo cadenza, it would have disturbed the cosmic, anoxic peace.

Whose Name Was Writ in Water

Womb is fluid for mosquito as well. Adrift with two air tubes that puncture the surface,the larva molts in a state that is paradisiacal. When it hatches, a mosquito pushes up through birth-scabbard waxen like a toe's callous after a swim. Mosquito stretches towards sunlight, flits from liquid tarmac, and prickles an afterimage which the water wimples, erases.

Field Trip

The trip I have yet to take,
where crows crumble,
where the transit of clouds steams
from a soil of mucid meat;
I will no longer discern
sun from moonlight, my
memories clinging
to branches shaped like
burst blood vessels in the eye,
and a leathery retinue,
beggars, kings, jesters, a child
holding the bone fingers
of her suicide mother,
will approach me,
each extending a torch,
black fire casting purple light,
guiding me across the
fields that resemble nothing
from the nothing in my nightmares.
How do I breathe, clear
my throat, or dip
my bread in gravy
and chew, when there are so,
so many thorns
already sticking in my gullet?

Chihuahua Desert

First Vision

Believe that granite is soluble, that
prickly pear yearns for skin and teeth.
Believe chaparral blooms in the brain when
rain wears a cracked arroyo. Believe
the jackrabbit scurries over sand to sniff
jagged strips of night, and that these
words sweat dust, that the sky
pours indigo over the desert while
the moon calcifies your thirst.

Second Vision

This is the death of wind,
this the bone of prayer and taste of tin –
here, thorn pierces the tongue of water,
teeth of dust chew cactus and weed,
heat secretes an enamel shell, heat
lays its eggs in the granite of sand,
here, sky is the bluest shade of fire,
and dew is the fourth mystery
in transubstantiation.

A Sleepless Man Sits Up in Bed

He stares at his hands, senses the obscure
galleys, coasts and watchtowers the dark
stretches across the open sea. There
is a light he has now lost: the glint
on a newly minted token, the sparkle
in an upraised glass as a boy drinks,
summer of parched weeds, a peeled orange
and white teeth, a door opened to
the patio where it is always noon.
Now in his bare room, as the house
grips down into the soil, and the wind
drags dawn over the hills to the villages
forsaken but for the elderly and black dogs,
he can no longer discern the source
of an endless creaking in the night:
The weather-vane? Or hull of the final ferry?

Sweat

Desert Winds, why did you give me
hands brimming with heat?
Everything I touch burns,
every palm frond becomes seared,
flutters up to the sun, like moths
swarming over the light
of a man praying in the dark.
I seek somewhere so northern
my skin will turn to glass,
and among the green snow-pines,
I will hear the wind click
new consonants from icicles.
Let me freeze so that twilight
may gurgle faucet's water
cold enough to shatter teeth.
Let me hear what dust doesn't register:
the bubbles and coolness as water stirs awake.
All the jugs of sand, all
the black dogs leaping and thirsty
will crystalize into an Arctic season beneath starlight.
Desert Winds, why did
you give me these hands full of fire?

Habituated

A beast hunkers in my fist
and shivers when fingers open.

I snuff his fire in a forest
where wolves sniff afterbirth,
crack the bones, and chew flesh
pooled atop beds of pine.

Or slowly, with the patience
of a mole sniffing for light, or water
rising through roots until reaching leaf,
I warm his breath within me.

My chest trembles, not
from chill, not grief, simply
the beast shaking the bars, pacing
the dirt floor of his cage.

He is what licks hands from the other side of knowing.
He is the black tongue and singed paw.
Come peer a cold eye. Feed him. You must.

Urge

To remain inside the hot earth was my wish.
A spider-shaped sun dragged me into her burrow of magma;
I didn't know baptisms, weddings, executions,
the streamers snapping in the wind, nor cared for those who survey
dunes, river and stones with theodolites and treaties.

I rooted deep within her entrails.

But the chamber burst, a conduit shot me up
amid rain, birdcall, shrieks and lightning-hot veins,
and I answered the sudden prick of air
with a sinewy life of teeth, nails and unforgiving snakes.

Border Town Graduates

Although we're closer to feeling the grass
pulled over our lips forever,
we still bare our dirty teeth and laugh.

We managed to look twice our age,
and now our wrinkles
won't be scraped from our mugs
when we're given our final shave.

Such is the residue
near motels and train tracks;
such is the cost,
lacking coolants in this desert.

Our moon was a pile of bones,
and our sun a blazing spider.

When thirsty,
we savored the taste
of her venom drunk hot.

Radiation

My life: the scroll unraveling
across atrium of a great temple.

It charts the circuitous
trail from human on asphalt to
human in cave to ape to rodent to amphibious
lizard slinking through
pumice rocks and leaving a mucus trail in which
cells evaporate into the
darkness where lifetimes click anew
under a different sun or
under no sun at all and
no lifetime at all but a fleck of helium adrift
in the palpable void between two solar systems.

I don't belong to this world or the adjacent;

I don't belong and
that's the thunder...

Pope Gregory the First

You whose hands are plumes of sulfur
Whose fingers press rivers of arsenic in wax-sealed mandates
Whose eye sockets contain orbs of bacterial aspic
Whose teeth dribble the distorted lexicon of the vulgate
Whose patriarchy is a cave of spiders
Whose loathing simmers in the milk of hypocrisy
Whose mercy is the locked ghetto
Whose benevolence would stitch foreskins to the circumcised

By forestalling the masses and
Their worship of the blood libel
With an edict of tolerance so that

The Jew would subsist on your electuary
Of acrid charity
Would drink from your teats dribbling vinegar
Would rest on a throne of thorns

His tenuous safety
Poisoned by spectral crime he didn't commit

Origin of the Non-Species

The hair of the dead is stirring;
shape of Crab-Nebulae,
or corolla of ejecta left after
the impact of a meteor,
their hair spreads through bushes,
slides over the grass, shockwaves
of electricity
flittering inside me like tapeworms.

Buried in sky,
I sink to the Earth from
a burning cloud;
threads of my spit,
my eye-veins, my fingers
solder into that web
of hair, mounds of earth
bellying up, spinnerettes
pissing hair-silk through burst stratum...

I plummet with bonewings
of an extinct raptor,
I emit the erasure of a howl
from a dire-wolf's dissolved larynx,
I melt from tail to lizard's wattle
and leave a blackmoist stain,
I curl into the inksack
of an octopus
which has evacuated
its melanin
then shriveled...

until I unbecome
first hydrogen, then
oxygen suctioned
into Darkwomb.

Battery

In the paintings of Francis Bacon
life-pulse is battery

bodily fluids gone awry
seepage of sourness
thru cheese-cloth

flesh burns
teeth flash like the snarling
muzzle of a chained guard-dog

in a drawing room
the suitor is stripped
and writhes with his double

they wrestle
sinews taut
pores oozing hunger
nostrils sniffing
sugar and decay in the red air and

meat perfume
on the tongues which flicker

and taste

agitated

shifting

Saying Goodbye to Carthage

I must go now.

I snip this cord of acetylene,
I mount the horse of sulfur and hydrogen,
dispatch telegrams of frost-crusted roses to the desert,
sink in a goblet of sky, braid
hair of the wind, dabble
with explosives that taste like tamarind
and vomit the elasticity of milk &
pour the blue syrup of siesta.

I will pack my bags and wait at the platform
for the train that roars through the fireplace,
and sleep the long journey to
the attic where
lyres are tuned and all dogs happy.

My skein of blood unravels through another border.
Goodbye to the skins of wine I kissed,
goodbye to the hot grottos adrift in smoke,
goodbye to the women who never wrote me, the stars
that leapt under my skin, the shadows
rustling like silk when each door I opened
revealed breasts and cunt
turned into a pillar of iodine.
Once I felt the moon jump in my veins,
(I wrote a haiku about this but it got lost).
Once I saw balloons released in a plaza
braided with the steam of meat and vendors,
once the water pipes clanked in the boarding house
while the city lit fireworks, and adulterers &
young lovers undressed in rooms jagged with crimson light,

(joy can easily fit in a bed with clean sheets).

But goodbye to your green-and-white taxi cabs,
I must depart.
Goodbye to your markets where trays
of meat stink the canned burn of menstruation, goodbye
to your produce of severed love, your beauty
like slit foreskins on a pushcart at noon, wasps churring,
goodbye to your recesses of marble & gold faucet bathrooms.

The desert gains another inch,
and there is no hay to harvest. Hard skies portend
blue edge of nightmare will cut your dreams,
botch your autopsies,
and toss an appendix in the almoner's cup.
Because I deny your watermelons and dust,
(I couldn't care less),
I cut all strings never attached, and say
goodbye to your gymnasiums and diners,
I foreclose this scrap of light,
crumble your cathedral with a pinch of salt.
Not a peso will be
sweat on interest accrued.

(I must leave now).

The assassin is hungry.

Funeral Song On The Death of Joaquín Pasos

By Carlos Martínez Rivas, translated from Spanish

1

With a snare-drum's rattling roll,
in the middle of a small *Plaza de Armas*,
as if for the obsequies honoring a hero... that's
how I would wish to commence. For just as
Death's Rite dictates that I forget his death,
I shall return to his life,—
and to those of other extinguished heroes who once
flared forth as he did down here.
For many are the young poets who have long since died.

Through the centuries they hail one another; we hear
their voices ignite, like roosters crowing then
answering from night's umbrage.
We know little about them: that they were young and tread
upon this earth. That they knew how to pluck the strings
          of an instrument.

That they felt the sea-breeze tousle their hair,
and contemplated the hills. That they loved a girl,
and that they clung to this fancy so tenaciously as to forget her.
That they wrote of it all, far too late, revising much
and one day died. Already their voices flame at night.

2

However, Joaquín, we know
much about you. I know... I travel back
to that day when in the embrace of your nanny
you suddenly became aware you existed.

And through this self-discovery you and your eyes were,
and your vision was the clearest that as yet any
being had attained. But you merely observed
with a stupefied, fateful gaze,
never retaining people for love or for hate.
(Even your small hands were more capable than others
at grasping an object, and not dropping it.)
One morning they took you to the barber's where
they solemnly sat you down; throughout the ordeal
your behavior was like a little gentleman's...
even though the customers poked fun at you,
even though the close clippers snipped your curls,
transforming you.
Later you hit the street. That other street
and other age when you scribble
a mustache across Leonardo's Mona Lisa,
when you're unkempt and uncouth...
but radiant youth soon bursts forth.
Later, we all know the rest: the toll
things took on you. The flow of beings
that pressed to meet you, each in turn
posing their questions
you had to answer with a clear
name which would resonate distinctly in their ears
among all others, just as we know
that the darkest men visited
Iaokanann in order to receive a name
so that henceforth
God could call upon them in the desert.
Thereafter, your destiny was such that you
could never gaze upon the earth,—
a nasty business, Joaquín. You learned
that before all things you paused to contemplate,
all were meted out an allotted time, and you would tremble.
That merely looking at them for

a reasonable time was enough to turn them
into something dreadful:
                              the blinding flash of a lemon.
The dull weight of an apple.
The pensive face of man.
The two breasts, pale and panting, heaving
beneath the blouse of a girl who's just run.
The hand that reaches out to touch her. Even words themselves...
everything had an essence inside itself. A sense
that resided at the core, unmoving, repeating itself,
neither waxing nor waning,
always full of its self, like a number.
And this list of names, this sum total you must
calculate for the day of reckoning,
and when you complete the calculation you shall become it.
Because they too gave you a name, so that
you would fill it with all, as in a crystal goblet.
So in such a manner you would include inside of you
starry nights, flowers,
village roofs seen from the road,
and that by uttering its name you would name yourself:
the sum total of all you saw.
To accomplish which they gave you only words,
verbs and some vague rules. Nothing tangible.
Not a single utensil like those that scrubbing
has made so shiny. And so I think
perhaps – just like me at times – you would've rather been a painter.
Painters at least have things. Brushes
to clean and keep in jars
of china and clay which they've purchased.
Paint-stained artifacts and all the objects
a simple man has devised for his own consolation.
Or to be a woodworker
carving a dancing nymph on furniture so that
the air actually ruffles her cloak.

But it's certain no man
ever controlled his destiny. And that difficult
labor turned you into the most honorable
type I know. Granted,
you knew what you were getting yourself into.
You saw workers as they go to the store. You watched
how they examine tools, test blades,
finally choosing the only one among the many: the wife
for the high bed of the construction scaffold.
Such was how you chose an adjective,
a word, and how you scanned a line;
you stalked as you would an enemy.
To make a poem was to plan the perfect crime.
It was to scheme a stainless lie,
made true by dint of purity.

3

And now you have died. And the flow of grace along with you.
It is said God has never permitted what
burns brightly among mortals to splutter, and fade.
Because of that our hope endures.
It's difficult to fight against the muddy
Olympus of the frogs. From earliest childhood they're
trained in the practice of nothing.
It is a great toil that the rest
shall be discerned. And yet there are few who
recognize it amid the smoke and jeers.
But we shall persevere, my dear Joaquín. Never fear.
And if by dying you have committed any treason,
that's your affair;
I shall not be one to judge you,
myself a frequent traitor.
Therefore,
I don't raise my voice against Death.

Poor maiden, always overwhelmed by her own power,
and embarrassed by the lamentations bursting over the corpse.
Only you can know your own death.
Its enigma doesn't concern the living, only life does.
While we are alive let Her be forgotten as if we were eternal.
And let us strive.
You, rooster of the Orco, awaken us.

4

And just as the bees of Thebes flew —
as old Elyan tells the tale — to suck honey from young Pindar's lips,
let this song stretch, touching your pallid head;
let it light on your breasts, piercing
your mouth with its own, quenching its fire-thirst;
let it flutter around your brow, weaving an
invisible crown upon your head.
Let its wings beat with increasing force, soaring
to greater heights with majestic turns.
Let it urge forth. Once more, and again,
describing greater and greater circles
in its flight towards the empyrean.

To the Reader

Whether or not
you speak the grain
of oak bark weathered
the gray of elephant;
or the stirring
of ants in a dead possum;
whether or not
you, a praise of flesh
through which the first verb burns,
know the smokewebbed
canals of sleep;

you
brighter than raised
glass of ale, you
sweet rankness of
roasted boar, you
greater than corn,
united with wheat, you

are a voice,
a breath
carving the curve
of an O, blade
honing impossible sand
into the circle of water;

you are the fleeting
element between
stone & flint, and
red air
conjugated in the
first person plural.

Anthony Seidman
is the author of two previous
collections of poetry: *On Carbon-Dating Hunger* and
Where Thirsts Intersect, both published by The Bitter
Oleander Press. With artist Jean-Claude Loubières, he
has created three artist's books: *When You Read...*,
San Fernando Valley Suite and *The Motel Insomnia*, all
published in bilingual format by *AdèLéo* of Paris, France.
His poems, articles and translations have appeared
widely in Mexico in such publications as *Luvina, Crítica,
Parteaguas*, the cultural supplements to Mexico's major
newspapers: *La Jornada* and *La Reforma*, and in *El blues
del cuervo* (Piedra Cuervo Press of Tijuana, Mexico),
translations from the poetry of Roberto Castillo
Udiarte. His translation and poems have been included
in the anthologies *Corresponding Voices* (Point of Contact
/ Syracuse University), *The Ecopoetry Anthology* (Trinity
University Press), *The California Prose Directory* (Outpost
19), and *Asymmetries: An Anthology of Peruvian
Poetry* (Cardboard House Press). He has recently
published work in *Bengal Lights, Cardinal Points Literary
Journal, Huizache, Drunken Boat, Nimrod, World Literature
Today, The Black Herald, The Bitter Oleander,* and *Chiron
Review*. Seidman resides in his native city of Los Angeles
with his wife and two children.

Nicaragua is a country
which has produced some of the most
important poetry in the Spanish language.
Rubén Darío and Salomón de la Selva are two
well-known examples. The poet Joaquín Pasos
(May 14, 1914 – January 20, 1947) is a poet who is
revered in his country, yet his poetry has not been
widely translated. His long poem 'Canción de guerra
de las cosas' rivals such open sequences of Latin
American poetry as *Luna Park* by Cardoza y Aragón,
and *Altazor* by Huidobro. His countryman and friend,
Carlos Martínez Rivas (1924-1998), was the author of
one major collection of poetry, *La insurrección solitaria*
(1953), and is one of the supreme poets of Nicaragua.
His 'Funeral Song On The Death of Joaquín Pasos'
is a sobering *ave atque vale* to his fellow poet,
and a meditation on the meaning of poetry,
a veritable *ars poetica*.

 **EYEWEAR** PUBLISHING